Original title:
Sunlight and Soil

Copyright © 2025 Creative Arts Management OÜ
All rights reserved.

Author: Sebastian Whitmore
ISBN HARDBACK: 978-1-80581-712-3
ISBN PAPERBACK: 978-1-80581-239-5
ISBN EBOOK: 978-1-80581-712-3

The Bright Frontier of Root and Bloom

In the garden where laughter plays,
Worms wiggle in their squishy ways,
Plants wear hats made of leafy green,
While flowers dance like they've seen a queen.

The carrots gossip, oh what a sight,
While radishes blushing, run from the light,
Beans are climbing with all their might,
Attempting to reach the clouds in flight.

A lazy sunflower begins to sway,
Dreaming of games in a bright ballet,
But a pesky bee buzzes in with cheer,
Saying, "Let's party! The fun's right here!"

Underneath, the rootlings twist and shout,
With little radishes jumping about,
It's a festival, it's oh-so-great,
Where veggies take turns at a plate of fate!

The Vibrance of Life against the Tilled

Nature wears boots, oh so bright,
Dancing around in the morning light.
Worms are the dancers, quick on their feet,
Cheering on plants with a rhythmic beat.

Each blade of grass knows a silly joke,
While peas in their pods giggle and poke.
Rabbits are laughing, bouncing with glee,
At carrots who wish they could run like the bee.

Twilight's Gift to the Growing Field

The moon winks softly, in a playful cheer,
As crickets croon tunes that all critters hear.
Tomatoes blush red, with rumors to spread,
While radishes plot schemes in a garden bed.

Even the crows have a dance to do,
With flappy wings and a silly coo.
A scarecrow grins at the mischief abound,
While daisies laugh at the antics around.

Gleaming Horizons in the Embracing Dirt

In patches of green, a party unrolls,
With dancing roots and muck-loving souls.
A funny old hedgehog spins round and round,
While bumblebees buzz out a jolly sound.

Mushrooms wear hats, all silly and swirled,
Inviting the bugs to join in the world.
Earthworms debate who's the fastest of all,
While grasshoppers leap to a banjo's call.

Nature's Quiet Celebration of Life

In the quiet of dawn, the creatures awake,
Mulching their plans for a wild frolic break.
A squirrel on stilts gives a comedic show,
While daisies giggle at his wobbling toe.

The breeze tells stories, all funny and bright,
As butterflies flutter, painting the night.
Each little critter, with a wink and a jest,
Cheers to the fun in their loamy fest.

Evergreen Dreams in Brightness

In a forest full of glee,
The trees gossip like they're on a spree.
They swap their leaves, a vibrant dance,
While squirrels chase, not missing a chance.

The sun winks through the leafy mask,
As critters play their merry task.
A badger raps, a rabbit hums,
And all join in with silly drums.

A Tapestry of Gleam and Grain

In fields of gold, the roosters crow,
But clucks and honks steal the show.
A pig in shades does a little jig,
While cows applaud, it's all quite a gig!

The corn does sway, a merry band,
As nature's choir sings hand in hand.
With bright green grass, the sheep all bleat,
Their woolly fluff can't hide their beat!

The Sway of Vibrant Life

In the garden, plants have fun,
With carrots dancing, oh what a run!
Tomatoes blushing, feeling bold,
As peppers yell, "We're pure gold!"

The bees do cha-cha, buzzing near,
While ants march proudly with no fear.
A flower tries to take a bow,
But the wind just laughs, "Not now, not now!"

Where Heaven Meets the Earth

In the meadow, laughter flies,
Butterflies chuckle with sparkling sighs.
A dog rolls down in sunny rays,
While grasshoppers hop in funny ways.

With daisies nodding in a breeze,
A rabbit sneezes, "Oh, oh geez!"
While clouds peek down, they're having fun,
It's a lively party under the sun!

Shades of Dawn and Earth

A rooster crowed, the sky turned pink,
The garden worm said, "Grab a drink!"
A radish giggled, shook with glee,
"I'm not a carrot, just wait and see!"

The flowers danced, they wore their best,
While ants hustled, on a tiny quest.
"Can you believe the bugs are back?"
"Yep, let's hide, and plan an attack!"

Vitality in Every Ray

A bumblebee buzzed with a grin,
"Hello there flower, where you been?"
The daisies rolled their petals wide,
"Come join the party, don't be shy!"

The daisies chatted, oh what a scene,
"One day I'm red, the next I'm green!"
A weed chimed in, "You're colored wrong!"
"Oh hush, dear weed, you're just not strong!"

Glorious Touch of the Celestial

A cloud passed by with a snooty stare,
"I'm on a diet, don't you dare!"
The sun peeked down, with a cheeky laugh,
"More fluffy muffins, that's my staff!"

The breeze strolled in with a playful pout,
"Why's everyone grumpy? Let's dance about!"
A leaf twirled down, on a whim,
"Catch me if you can, just on a limb!"

The Beneath and the Above

The worms below held a secret feast,
"Tonight we dine on roots, at least!"
A bug above rolled on the grass,
"You guys can't cook, you're such a class!"

The stars twinkled, added a cheer,
"What's the dirt doing? Come up here!"
The ants shouted back, "It's real estate!"
"We move in style, just wait and rate!"

Echoes of Light and Life

In the sky, the twinkle's gleam,
Flowers dance, or so it seems.
A squirrel steals a seed with glee,
Joking with the buzzing bee.

Worms in coats of earthy brown,
Laugh as they churn beneath the ground.
Roots tickle toes of sneaky bugs,
While ants form trains, all snug as rugs.

The sun spills laughs on leaves above,
Every blade a tale of love.
A dandelion, with a grin,
Winks at clouds that drift like kin.

So here we are, with hearty cheer,
Nature's stage is crystal clear.
Amidst this game of light and cheer,
Who knew the dirt could bring such cheer!

The Flourish of Fresh Beginnings

From tiny seeds to giants, bloom,
In every corner, there's room.
Ladybugs wear their polka dots,
While grasshoppers dance in parking lots.

The early risers stretch and yawn,
In vibrant colors, they don dawn.
Beetles march with little drums,
To the rhythm of the garden's hums.

Puddles splash with gleeful cries,
As raindrops fall from giggly skies.
Every sprout sings funny tunes,
As rabbits hop beneath the moons.

In the dirt, there's joy galore,
Twirling leaves on the forest floor.
Every bud brings laughter's ring,
Oh, what fun the seasons bring!

Golden Streams on Earth's Canvas

A painter's brush, the sky's bright hue,
Bounces off the petals, too.
Butterflies wear wings of grace,
Each one flaunts a funny face.

Grass blades peek with silly grins,
Cheering on the tiny fins.
Fish in puddles, doing flips,
Cracking jokes with watery quips.

Sun-chased giggles fill the air,
Petals sway without a care.
A chubby toad croaks a cheer,
While drumming frogs keep time, oh dear!

Nature's stage is full of fun,
Every moment, just begun.
So let's dance in the warm embrace,
Of this lively, lovely place!

Warm Embrace of the Waking Land

Caught in a hug of morning dew,
Bumblebees sip like they're at the brew.
Flowers gossip about the breeze,
As ants march past with cheesy ease.

Twisting vines and whirling ferns,
Have their own eccentric turns.
Silly roots play hide and seek,
With the stones, they twist and peek.

Chickens chuckle as they strut,
While rabbits nibble on their rut.
The soil grins beneath the play,
Cheering on this wild ballet.

With every bloom, comes a jest,
In this land that's nature's best.
So let's raise a toast, my friend,
To the mirth that will never end!

A Tangle of Green and Glimmering Gold

In the garden, gnomes do jig,
They dance around, not quite so big.
With every plant that stretches tall,
They plot to steal a veggie ball.

The carrots giggle, peas play pranks,
While radishes wear funny clanks.
The bees buzz in with great delight,
For pollen parties last all night.

A daisy dons a silly hat,
While worms compose a jazzy spat.
The earthworms twist in rhythmic rolls,
As daisies stomp on garden goals.

At dusk they strike their final pose,
The garden laughs, it surely knows.
A tangle here, a tangle there,
With glimmering dreams afloat in air.

Beneath a Sky of Glowing Wonder

Beneath the hue of orange hue,
A squirrel chats with a friendly shrew.
The clouds, they giggle, fluff on fluff,
While kittens frolic, just too tough.

The shadows stretch, they play charades,
As flowers don their finest grades.
The bumblebees begin to hum,
While ants march by in military drum.

A rainbow slides on a baby's face,
As critters dance about the place.
They tumble, trip, and shout hooray,
For this grand show on bright display.

At twilight's call, the stars align,
The critters toast with sparkling wine.
Beneath this sky so full of cheer,
They laugh out loud, for spring is here.

Illumined Trails of Growth and Dream

In meadows bright, we'll take a ride,
On bouncy frogs, they jump with pride.
The daisies cheer, they clap their leaves,
As butterflies wear sassy sleeves.

The path ahead is filled with glee,
Where dandelions guide the spree.
The ladybugs share silly tales,
As friendly worms ride bike-sized trails.

The mushrooms giggle, polka-dot,
While roots engage in a tickle plot.
The sun, it winks, a knowing gleam,
As all things shimmy in the dream.

At night they sing, a lilting tune,
Their laughter echoes, bright as moon.
With twinkling stars above so near,
In trails of growth, delight is here.

Embraced by the Day's Gentle Kiss

The rooster crows, a wild surprise,
As chickens strut in fancy ties.
The beds of spinach start to sway,
As radishes shout, 'We rule the day!'

The sun peeks through the curtain blur,
While the frog croaks tunes that start to stir.
The daisies wear their best attire,
As critters dance around the fire.

A cat in boots begins to spin,
While mushrooms laugh in their own skin.
The worms are poets, crafting rhymes,
As garden humor grows in climes.

With each new bud that starts to sprout,
The joyous chorus swells about.
Embraced by light, a perfect bliss,
With giggles shared, no gloom to kiss.

Reflections of Brilliance in the Earth

In morning's glow, the world awakes,
A worm hits snooze, for goodness' sakes!
Grass decides to rock a funky dress,
While ants are planning their own success.

Bees buzz about, with snacks to share,
Dancing with flowers, they show off flair.
A chicken trips on a farmyard joke,
While pigs just laugh and start to smoke.

Rays that Stir the Hidden Roots

The shady shrub begins to giggle,
As toddlers jump and do a wiggle.
The roots below, they're feeling bold,
Calling out, 'We've stories untold!'

Caterpillars host a wild parade,
While scaredy-mice switch to charades.
A vulture's eye-roll, oh what a scene!
While daffodils strut in shades of green.

A Symphony of Light and Land

The cauliflowers hum a jaunty tune,
While cabbages dance underneath the moon.
Potatoes grumble, stuck in their spot,
Complaining about the party—what a plot!

Chickens rap in the early morn light,
While carrots dream of a daring flight.
A tree gets tickled by a playful breeze,
Shrugging off worries with laughable ease.

The Caress of Day in The Dark Richness

A mole emerged with a puzzled air,
As daisies giggled without a care.
Kick back, and let the grass blades sway,
Nothing like fun on a leafy playday!

Earthworms flirt with a wormy dance,
While beetles steal every last glance.
Pigeons perch, gossiping away,
While worms shout, 'Hey, check out our clay!'

Captured Light in Green Halls

In the garden, thrillers play,
The veggies dance, hip-hop sway,
Beets wear shades, carrots groove,
While lettuce shimmies, in the move.

A tomato leaps to catch a ray,
Squirrels roll and join the fray,
Peas in pods, they laugh and cheer,
Count the clouds, just look—oh dear!

Radishes wear polka dots,
Mischief lurks in every plot,
Cabbages snack on morning dew,
While dancing beans scream, "Look at you!"

As the bunnies hop around,
In this hilarity, joy is found,
A celebration of the bright,
As green and giggles take their flight.

Harmony of Brightness and Roots

In a patch where veggies dream,
Cucumbers plot a sneaky scheme,
Carrots giggle, onions sigh,
Tomatoes wonder, 'Oh, why not fly?'

Radishes tell the best jokes,
While zucchini pulls some funny folks,
They laugh as they sip their dew,
Squeezing jokes from clouds of blue.

Potatoes in sunglasses strut,
Joining in with a cheeky nut,
Chilis dance like party kings,
Spinning tales and silly things.

Beets sing songs of winning pairs,
Leeks declare their love for fairs,
Basil twirls, what a delight,
In this ground, all feels so right!

Gentle Caress of Day

As laughter wakes the morning cheer,
Radishes shout, 'Come over here!'
A leafy dance in the gentle breeze,
Merriment grows among the peas.

The carrots play a game of hide,
While seedlings waddle side by side,
With quirky moves and silly grins,
They twirl with joy, let the games begin!

"Rhubarb, don't trip!" a shout resounds,
While broccoli bounces, hops and bounds,
In this patch of quirky fun,
The day is bright, and they have won.

As the sun sets low, they sigh,
Beneath the sky they laugh and try,
For the night brings dreams of play,
In their home, they dance away!

Radiant Canopy and Beneath

Underneath the leafy cheer,
A garden party, come and steer,
Peppers juggle, squash boats float,
While plants embrace, opinions gloat.

The roots below, they whisper tales,
Of sneaky snails and bouncing bales,
"Lettuce needs a spa today,"
While beet greens plan a wild foray.

Petunias gossip, spreading lore,
Of radish dreams and garden score,
With every wiggle and a dive,
They lay the fables, keeping alive.

As day ends, the fun persists,
In this earth, they twist and twist,
With every chuckle, every glee,
Life beneath is a comedy!

Bright Blossoms in Rich Embrace

In the garden, flowers wink,
They dance around, don't you think?
With petals bright, they play a game,
Competing for the sun's warm flame.

A bee buzzes, thinking he's suave,
But accidentally hits a lave!
The blooms giggle, rolling in cheer,
While ants march on, without any fear.

Thanks to mud that likes to hug,
Each shoot stands up, feeling snug.
They laugh at the weeds, oh so bold,
"Your fashion sense just makes us cold!"

So come for a stroll where laughter grows,
Among the friends with bright colored clothes.
They bloom and sway in a jolly spree,
A festival of joy, oh can't you see?

A Palette of Gold upon the Black

In the plot where laughter thrives,
Golden peeks and playful dives.
Painted leaves with polka dots,
Giggling stems in amusing spots.

A squirrel tips, oh what a sight!
He nibbles seeds and takes flight.
With every leap, he steals a show,
While down below, the daisies glow.

The ballet of grass, they sway and twirl,
In a party where everyone's a pearl.
Twirling vines with a quirky bend,
Join the fun, it's a trend to lend!

Colors burst like laughter here,
Tickling toes, spreading cheer.
Stay a while in this grand display,
Where nature plays, come join the fray!

Bright Tides of Growth in a Quiet Soil

In the quiet where green dreams rise,
Tiny sprouts play peek-a-boo with the skies.
Each leaf whispers tales of cheer,
As worms wiggle, full of beer!

Dandelions laugh with fluffy heads,
They shout to the wind, "We're party threads!"
Grumpy thistles shake their fists,
"Why can't we join in on the trysts?"

A ladybug glides, dressed to impress,
While critters unite in this big, bold mess.
With giggles sprouting from every nook,
Even the mushrooms have a storybook.

So here in this space of warms and cool,
Nature's playground is the best kind of school.
Leaves and laughter, a jovial dance,
Join the fest, come take a chance!

The Harmony of Warmth and Ground

Underneath the skies so fair,
Seeds plot a giggle with flair.
They joke about the clouds up high,
"Can't reach us here, oh me, oh my!"

A broccoli dreams of a pizza slice,
While carrots do yoga, which is nice!
Beets blush at the jokes they throw,
While radishes giggle in a row.

The dance of roots, a tangled beat,
Tickling worms who can't find their seat.
Each sprout a comedian, oh what a sight,
In the jolly show of green delight.

So stroll through the laughter, say hi to the clan,
Where each quirky veggie has a colorful plan.
In this festival of life, come partake,
Grab a smile, take it home as a keepsake!

Vows of Brightness in the Gentle Soil

In the garden of giggles, worms dance about,
They swear to the daisies, with a twist and a pout.
The carrots are laughing, they're wearing a crown,
While peas play their trumpets, king of the town.

The tulips are gossiping, in colors so bright,
Telling tales of a snail who outran a kite.
With a wink and a nod, all the sprouts raise their cups,
Cheers to the sunbeams and earthworms in ruts.

Blossoms Singing in the Warmth of Day

Petals are prancing, singing songs in the breeze,
Fluffy clouds giggle, they're floating with ease.
A robin in a tuxedo, singing off-key,
Says, 'Who needs a concert? Just listen to me!'

The ivy's in stitches, it can't stop its climb,
While daisies debate who can rhyme the best rhyme.
With each giggle and chuckle, they sway to and fro,
In this sunlight-filled dance, they steal quite the show.

Glowing Threads Weaving Through the Earth

Raccoons in tuxedos toast underground vines,
While badgers in caps read their fancy designs.
The roots play charades, oh what a wild scene,
'I'm an onion!' yells one, 'Now can you guess green?'

The underground parties, they know how to groove,
With worms in the corner, busting out their moves.
As earthworms are twirling, the beetles applaud,
In a world full of laughter, no one is flawed.

The Breath of Growth in Waking Lumiere

Awake, said the daisies, with a movie premiere,
The sun spills its laughter, bringing cheer and good cheer.

The seedlings are ready, they've rehearsed all night,
Bringing jokes to the daisies, what a funny sight!

The butterflies waltz, in a dance so surreal,
While ants in tuxes hustle, with channeling zeal.
They debate who eats crumbs, but then they all share,
In this silly tale of growth, no one has a care.

Radiance on the Tilled Horizon

In fields where the veggies giggle and grow,
The carrots wear shades, putting on quite the show.
Tomatoes are blushing, they're red with delight,
While corn does the cha-cha, it's quite a sight!

The potatoes are raving, with dirt on their jeans,
They dance in the daylight, fueled by their dreams.
Eggplants are spinning, they're graceful and bold,
Their purple tops twirling like dancers of gold!

The radishes boast, 'We're the roots of the party!'
While lettuce just laughs, saying, 'Aren't we all hearty?'
Beets beat the drum as they rhythmically roll,
In this merry garden, we all play our role!

So come join the fun, where the laughter is free,
In the land of the leafy, we dance with glee.
With veggies that chatter and cheer all around,
We'll party together, let joy know no bound!

Nature's Brushstrokes in the Morning Glow

The flowers awake, in pj's so bright,
With sleepy-eyed bees buzzing, 'Is this daylight?'
Tulips are giggling, painting the scene,
While daisies share secrets, like a blooming queen!

The grass hums a tune, with blades all in line,
'We're tickled by feet, oh isn't it divine?'
Fern fronds play hide and seek, clever and sly,
As butterflies whisper, 'We'll give it a try!'

The clouds are the artists, with brushes so light,
They splash pastel colors, a flamboyant sight.
A squirrel in the branches, a clumsy ballet,
Falls splat on the ground—'Hey, is it lunch break today?'

With laughter and shapes, the day starts anew,
In nature's fine gallery, the joy is so true.
Each petal a canvas, each leaf a delight,
We paint with our laughter from morning to night!

Luminous Whispers Beneath the Stars

At dusk, when the critters come out for a chat,
The owls tell the jokes, and the rabbits laugh fat.
Fireflies are blinking like starlit confetti,
While crickets recite poetry—real classy and petty!

The moon casts a grin, a light cheeky and wide,
The night sky says, 'Hey, let's enjoy the ride!'
A fox in a tux makes a formal debut,
While raccoons juggle snacks, all sticky yet cute!

Beneath the bright canvas where dreams start to twirl,
Each star has a story, as they softly swirl.
The night is a comic, with antics galore,
Where every critter's a character—not a bore!

So gather your friends, take a moment to spar,
In this quirky night world, so splendid, bizarre!
With giggles and sparkle, let whispers take flight,
Beneath twinkling wonders, we dance through the night!

The Dance of Brilliance and Ground

Oh, dance, dance, the flora and fauna, they say,
The daisies do waltz, with the moss leading the play.
With each little petal that sways to the beat,
The thorns tap their toes, not missing a feat!

The mushrooms do disco—they're quite a sensation,
While ants form a line for the grand celebration.
The trees sway their branches, in robes of bright green,
As the dandelions scatter, a whimsical scene!

With laughter in petals, and glee in the air,
Each plant has a joke; oh, we're all here to share!
The butterflies spin like confetti on wing,
While ladybugs laugh, crowned as the spring king!

The soil gives a chuckle, the worms twist and shout,
In this joyful ballet, there's never a doubt.
As we dance with the breezes, the moments are clear,
In this wild, earthy party, there's nothing to fear!

Resonance of Rays in Earthen Embrace

In the garden, a radish sings,
While carrots jest in their orange bling,
Tomatoes laugh with a squishy grin,
As peas play tag, let the fun begin.

A worm nods off on a leafy breeze,
Sharing jokes with the buzzing bees,
Chuckle with roots, buried deep below,
As flowers dance in the warm, soft glow.

Underneath a zucchini's big hat,
A cucumber dreams, 'Oh, how about that!'
With greens having a giggle, oh what a show,
In this earthy realm, there's always a flow.

Mushrooms whisper in caps of delight,
While broccoli joins with a merry bite,
Together they spout little jokes galore,
In this thriving patch, you can't help but roar!

A Song of Green Cradled in Light

The lettuce croons in a leafy dress,
While peas in a pod share their best guess,
A sunflower winks, it's never too proud,
Tickling the breeze, it giggles out loud.

Radishes roll like they're on parade,
While sprouts poke fun at the lemon jade,
Cabbages chuckle with rouged cheeks bright,
A veggie jamboree, what a delight!

As bees zippity-zoom through the patch,
The carrots play leapfrog, oh what a match,
Dancing around in the splash of the day,
In this green concert, come join the fray!

The herbs are gossiping, twirling about,
Basil tells thyme, "What's that fuss all about?"
In nature's laughter, all worries take flight,
Cradled in warmth, oh, what pure light!

Recipes of Growth Hidden from View

A tomato whispers a secret dish,
While onions giggle, they can't make a wish,
Peppers chime in with a spicy remark,
As radishes rustle in a bright red park.

Sneaky beans plot in their wriggly way,
Saying, "Let's make it a veggie buffet!"
Squashes go soft, with their tales to share,
While chives laugh loudly, shaking their hair.

The beets are plotting a grand masquerade,
Wearing their rouge, in shade they parade,
Under the surface, the roots have a ball,
Cooking new jokes for one and for all!

In this hidden world, there's plenty of cheer,
With laughter and growth that is loud and clear,
As nature concocts funny food for the stew,
These silly delights come alive just for you!

The Secret Beneath the Golden Touch

In the earth, where giggles reside,
A gopher will dance, trying to hide,
With carrots and radishes making a scene,
As they host a party, all crisp and green.

A hidden patch full of chuckles and cheer,
Where roots spill stories of laughter sincere,
Pumpkins roll over with glee in their shells,
As bunnies hop in with their funny yells.

Beneath what's blooming, the mischief unfolds,
As garlic and chives exchange playful holds,
With sunny-side up dreams, they chat and they cheer,
In their cozy abode, no worries to fear!

The ticket to fun is buried so deep,
In the quilt of the earth, where secrets still sleep,
So gather your giggles from all that you see,
For nature's the chef serving joy endlessly!

Sun-Kissed Dreams Buried Deep

In the garden where veggies conspire,
Radishes dance in their leafy attire.
They giggle and wiggle, plotting a scheme,
To pop up and tickle, that's their big dream.

Carrots in orange wear hats made of green,
Pretending they're all in a leafy cuisine.
Tomatoes are blushing, saying, 'Look at me!'
While cucumbers whisper, 'It's all just silly!'

The peas roll with laughter in pods all a'flutter,
As beans jump around like they're caught in some butter.
Beets wear their colors like crowns on their head,
While turnips just sigh, 'Can we go back to bed?'

Oh, the joy in the patch, a wild festive spree,
Where the flowers throw parties for folks like you and me.
They joke in the breeze, in the dirt they delight,
Wishing for snacks till the stars shine so bright.

Colors of Nourishment Underneath

Under the surface, a party's underway,
With radish diplomats gaining ground every day.
The potatoes in dresses scream, 'We're quite chic!'
While onions just layer it up with a peek.

Zucchinis are giddy, spinning round their patch,
Saying, 'Who knew being humble could be quite a catch?'
The peppers wear jackets, they brag and they boast,
While mushrooms just laugh, stealthy ghosts at the roast.

The lettuce is giggling, crisp as a crunch,
Saying, 'Let's form a parade, we can brunch!'
The herbs raise their voices, a fragrant bouquet,
In the soil's funny world, they cheer all day.

And when the sun sets, it's a festival scene,
With roots sharing stories of what might have been.
They chuckle and wiggle, all snug in their bed,
Excited for tomorrow, and more jokes to spread.

The Ground's Gentle Reach for the Light

In the garden, the ground tickles feet,
Reaching for rays in a dance that's so sweet.
Wiggly worms wear top hats, proud and stout,
While the daisies shout, 'What's this all about?'

Tomatoes, they blush in that warm, golden glow,
Saying, 'We're fashionistas, just look at our show!'
While peas pop and giggle, swinging and swinging,
The soil is grinning, oh, the joy it is bringing!

Beets are in bickering, debated in reds,
'Who steals the limelight? Look here at our heads!'
And carrots complain, 'Why so much chatter?'
'We're all soaking in rays, that's what really matters!'

In this lively domain, there's laughter galore,
Hands in the dirt, how could one ask for more?
As the stars start to twinkle, the critters all cheer,
For the ground's fun-filled reach brings the best of the year.

Jewel Tones of the Earth Encountering Bright

Oh, the jewels all sparkle, the colors collide,
The beans in their costumes are bursting with pride.
Red ones are bragging, 'We're vibrant and bold!'
While greens strut their stuff, wishing to be sold.

Pumpkins are plotting a round-up in style,
While cabbages roll, each with a sly smile.
Squash jokes and giggles from yellow to green,
In this carnival of colors, nature's queen.

Eggplants keep whispering fancy little schemes,
'Throw a bash for the veggies, fulfill all our dreams!'
Radishes retreat, 'We're tough, don't you see?'
While peppers just shimmer, a savor spree.

The dance of the garden, so merry and bright,
With roots swaying gently in soft, moonlit night.
When dawn breaks so cheerful, they hum in delight,
In this colorful world, it's a whimsical sight.

The Shimmering Canvas of Awakening Life

In the morning, the ground wears a coat,
Wrinkles and patches, what a funny quote!
Little critters dance with flair,
Worms in bowties, without a care.

The flowers giggle, they tickle the air,
With petals like hats, they rise without a scare!
Tiny ants march, all in their line,
Claiming the land, 'This patch is mine!'

Illuminated Wonders in the Earthen Layer

Underground parties, the moles all cheer,
With disco balls made of roots, oh dear!
Rabbits hop by with a stylish hop,
"Who wears it best?" they giggle and stop.

Sprouts do a dance while the beetles applaud,
Elves with their shovels say, 'Ain't this odd?'
With each little sprout, there's laughter galore,
As they plan their next neighborhood tour!

Gold and Green's Divine Confluence

A dandelion dressed in hues of gold,
Said to the grass, 'Are we getting old?'
The leaves laughed hard, swayed side to side,
'Let's throw a party, let's enjoy the ride!'

The sunbeams winked, played peek-a-boo,
while happy roots sang, 'We need coffee too!'
Buds blushing pink, all ready to sway,
"We're the best team, let's dance all day!"

A Tale of Radiant Growth and Richness

In the dirt, a potato thought it was hot,
'Is it me, or am I too much of a tot?'
Meanwhile, a carrot did a little spin,
'Don't fret, my friend, we're all bound to win!'

Turnips in tuxedos, prancing about,
'We're in the limelight, let's give a shout!'
With laughter and cheer, they made quite the scene,
In this jolly patch, happiness was seen!

Brightness upon the Sleeping Earth

There once was a rock with great dreams,
It thought it could dance, or so it seems.
But as it lay still, in the dirt quite deep,
The worms had a party, while it snoozed in sleep.

The ants wore tiny hats, full of flair,
While the grass giggled softly at the sight laid bare.
A ladybug DJ turned tunes on the leaf,
With beats that made even the soil feel relief.

Mice in the dark crept out to compete,
In joyous ballet with happy little feet.
But Mr. Stone snored loud, a terrible sound,
As earth's merry jesters spun around-town.

At last, when he woke from his snoozy parade,
He found that the fun left him quite dismayed.
So he rolled with a laugh, and joined in the spree,
For fun is much better with friends, don't you see?

Morning's Gift to the Seed Beneath

In the morning, a seed had a wish,
To sprout into something delicious to dish.
"I'll be a great veggie," it declared with glee,
While dreaming of salads and fancy green tea.

A rabbit in glasses heard this grand plot,
And chuckled, "Oh darling, why don't you sprout hot?
With butter and garlic, you'll surely delight,
Your goals seem too lofty, better sleep tight!"

But the seed was so eager to rise with the sun,
It tickled the dirt and began its fun run.
With roots like spaghetti and leaves like a cape,
It burst from the ground, a green superhero shape!

"Oh look! I'm quite fabulous!" it exclaimed,
While the rabbit just nodded, impressed and ashamed.
"Okay," said the hare, "your dreams weren't quite daft.
But I'm still best with dips, now that's quite a craft!"

The Alchemy of Glow and Ground

There once was a beet, or so it was said,
Who dreamed to be famous and earn lots of bread.
"I'll glow in the garden with glimmers of gold,
And soon I'll be known, a sight to behold!"

A potato laughed hard, with eyes all aglow,
"Good luck, my dear friend, it's hard to steal show.
With all that you're wishing, I'd suggest just be wise,
Roots are best hidden, with no need for disguise."

But the beet took its chance, with a sparkle and grin,
Caught the gopher's eye, and soon it began.
To dance in the moonlight, in carrot costume too,
While shouting, "I'm a veggie! Look at my hue!"

The garden erupted in giggles and cheers,
As the beet turned what's humble to great cavalier.
"Tonight, I will feast upon roasted delight,
And share my great story 'til next moonlit night!"

The Light-Filled Pathway to Growth

In a meadow so bright, the flowers did sway,
Two daisies debated who'd outshine the day.
"Oh lovely such petals, so white and divine,
But wait! Minuscule me has a role as well, fine!"

A dandelion whispered, "Don't blame your poor fate,
We all have our moments; it's never too late.
Let's host a grand party, throw blooms in the air,
Bring laughter and cheer—extreme solstice affair!"

So up went the petals, and who'd have a fuss?
As bees joined the dance, and the ants made a bus.
They celebrated life in a garish bouquet,
A carnival of colors to brighten the day!

As twilight approached, they bid their farewell,
Promising next spring they'd do this quite swell.
And so they grew vast, with a giggle and twirl,
In that light-filled realm, all they did was whirl!

The Pulse of Nature's Light

The beams peek in, a playful tease,
Dancing with ants, rustling leaves.
Worms practice yoga in their cozy holes,
While the grass giggles and sways like trolls.

Tiny seedlings throw a party in rows,
While shadows prance, striking silly poses.
Bees wear polka dots, buzz on parade,
And flowers blush with each cotton candy braid.

The ground grumbles, a ticklish affair,
As daisies wear hats, with a flair to spare.
Under this circus of photo shoots bright,
Nature's laughter echoes, oh what a sight!

With soil beneath, and green all around,
Every creature is lost in joy sound.
If you listen closely, you'll surely find,
Even the rocks have a joke in mind!

Interplay of Glow and Ground

The flickers tease, and shadows play,
Frogs in tuxedos hop all day.
Caterpillars frown, then burst out in cheer,
As every step brings giggles near.

Earthworms plot mischief under the bed,
While ladybugs haven't a worry in their head.
A squirrel with shades, strutting with pride,
Claims his throne on a branch, full of vibes.

The dance of rays gives beetles some sass,
As they strut their stuff across soft grass.
With flowers strumming their petal guitars,
This natural riot sings beneath the stars.

Oh, to frolic where mirth takes flight,
Where ants wear capes in the bliss of the night.
Every pebble wishes to join the fun,
In this land of giggles beneath the sun!

A Field of Illuminated Whispers

Glowing orbs peek, all around the field,
Grass tickles feet, magic is revealed.
Chasing shadows like playful ghosts,
Nature's giggle is what I love most.

Crickets dance in a debate so bold,
Arguing over who's the prettiest mold.
Fungus in bow ties struts down the lane,
While daisies trade hats and discuss the rain.

Each blade of green has a tale to tell,
Of bugs on bicycles, ringing a bell.
Soft whispers exchange their own little lore,
As the sun forgets, who knocked at the door.

In this realm where laughter blooms
Even the mushrooms wiggle in their rooms.
A symphony fat with joyous delight,
In a world of whimsy, all feels so right!

Dappled Dreams in Verdant Seas

Freckles of joy on a leaf's bright face,
Laughter lands lightly, leaves a trace.
Flower pot races, a riot of hues,
While bunnies in sunglasses sing the blues.

The ground cracks a grin at the grass's jokes,
And wary hedgehogs just poke their pokes.
Busy bees drop the beat for a dance,
As puddles reflect the glamour of chance.

A patch of carrots critiques a sweet sun,
"Get off our backs!" they exclaim, "We're done!"
While whispers of petals share tales of old,
Of the day the tomatoes were kissed by bold.

From roots that tickle to the sky that beams,
This garden's alive with whimsical dreams.
In every inch of this playful delight,
Nature's own comedy steals the night!

Glowing Pictures on the Earth's Palette

Beneath the sky's bright canvas wide,
The plants wear colors, full of pride.
Each leaf has flair, each sprout a style,
They dance around and laugh awhile.

Worms don their shades of earthy bold,
Fashion feels from treasures untold.
Rainbow greens and cheery browns,
In this garden, no one frowns.

A flower's grin, a vegetable laugh,
Together they create a vibrant graph.
Nature's artists, freely they play,
Merriment blooms in a funny way.

With giggles shared and roots that twist,
Each little plant has joys to list.
In cheeky shades, they spread the cheer,
The earth's bright palette, oh so dear!

Illumination of Growth Underneath

Digging below where the critters hide,
There lurk some potatoes, quite the ride.
They giggle and snicker, oh what a feat,
As roots get tangled, no one admits defeat.

The carrots chuckle in orange delight,
Wiggly worms join the party tonight.
Radishes blush, a red-rooted jest,
Beneath the surface, they love to fest!

With stories of soil and mud cakes to bake,
They share their secrets and laughter they stake.
The underground crew, such a cheeky bunch,
Meet me for dinner and crunchity munch!

As sprouts stretch higher, they plot and scheme,
Of veggie tales and a root-styled dream.
With every tickle of toes in the ground,
They giggle together, sweet laughter profound!

The Glow of Life Rising Upward

Petals peek out, with a wink and a shine,
Buds yell, "Hey, look! The world's really fine!"
While sprouts stretch tall, doing ballerina twirls,
The garden's a stage for dancing pearls.

Bumblebees buzzing, they join in the fun,
Mimicking flowers, they all try to run.
With whims in the air and pollen to play,
Nature's own circus brightens the day.

While nature grins in a show-offy way,
The sunbeams join in, just wanting to stay.
Plant pals are laughing, they can't keep it in,
"Glowy and happy, let's all spin and spin!"

As laughter erupts from the buds all around,
The earth's little children dance safe and sound.
With cheerful antics upon the green stage,
In this lively world, we all feel the rage!

Warm Hues in Silent Fertility

In stillness of morning, the colors arise,
Warm tones unspooling like joyful surprise.
Golden yellows and soft browns collide,
Creating a tapestry where giggles abide.

The green thumbs chuckle, wishing for rain,
Hoping for giggles from soft drops again.
Tiny sprouts whisper their plans to the wind,
With secretive smiles, their antics have sinned.

In the garden's hush, mischief unfolds,
As chili plants tease with tales to be told.
Nature's comedy blooms, with humor so bright,
Life's a big joke, in spots of pure light!

In this playful plot, where laughter is sown,
Every flower has secrets, and none are alone.
So tilt your head down, and peer in the ground,
For funny surprises are ready to be found!

Shimmering Rays through the Green Veil

Through a leafy cloak, giggles sneak,
A bright beam chuckles, oh so cheeky.
Plants whisper jokes to the gentle breeze,
While roots do the salsa, aiming to please.

Beams dance like children in a park,
Tickling the grass till it leaves its mark.
Worms, with their wiggles, join the parade,
As daisies laugh loud; they're not afraid!

A sunflower grins, a mischievous scene,
"Did you hear the one about the green bean?"
Laughter erupts from the daisies nearby,
While butterflies flutter, oh my, oh my!

Radiance turns grumpy sprouts into jest,
Life's garden party is truly the best!
Raise a glass to the glowing delight,
Where every little critter is out for a bite!

Nurtured by the Dawn's Gentle Touch

At dawn's early hour, it's party time,
The beans start breakdancing, what a rhyme!
Tiny leaves hop and do a jig,
While peas blow bubbles, oh so big!

The cucumber tumbles, oh what a sight,
A shot of morning cheer, what pure delight!
Gardeners chuckle, holding their tools,
As earthworms play hopscotch, breaking the rules.

Glorious sprouts, sway to a tune,
Singing sweet nothings under the moon.
Even the broccoli joins in the fun,
Waving its florets, "Aren't we number one?"

With laughter and giggles, the morning is bright,
Planning a feast under skies of blue light.
A symphony formed in the patch nearby,
Where veggies unite, oh my, oh my!

The Light That Kisses the Earth

A cheeky glow peeks from its slumber,
Tickling the petals, oh what a number!
Cabbages blush at the playful tease,
While carrots wiggle, aiming to please.

Lettuce giggles, a frosty delight,
As radishes pop up, ready for flight.
"They can't catch us!" they squeak with glee,
"Hide and seek, come play under the tree!"

A gleam rolls by, the daisies laugh loud,
Spouting silly jokes, proud of their crowd.
A pun-filled plot thickens in the patch,
Where every little greenery shares a match.

The light brings joy, that much is clear,
As everyone bustles, spreading the cheer.
In a world of color, where laughter's the root,
Who knew veggies could be such a hoot?

Awakening the Seedlings with Radiance

Awake, little sprouts, it's time for play,
The golden beams are here to stay!
"Shall we dance?" a sprout suggests,
As chubby potatoes start their quests.

Tomatoes giggle in their comfy beds,
Tickling the soil with laughter and spreads.
A dainty petunia sings in delight,
As herbs join the chorus, ready to bite!

Overhead, birds cheer, swooping down low,
With melodies sweet, they put on a show.
The dirt rolls around, a joyful ballet,
As every little plant comes out to play.

Like tiny comedians, they perform with flair,
Rusty old gardening tools stop and stare.
In the theater of green, the laughter is bold,
With every sprout laughing, the magic unfolds!

A Tapestry of Warmth and Root

In the garden, where veggies plot,
Broccoli wearing pants, what a thought!
Tomatoes dance in polka dot joy,
While carrots play hide and seek like a toy.

Rabbits meet for tea, oh what a scene,
Discussing the best way to munch on green.
While ladybugs wear tutus so bright,
They boogie all day, what a funny sight!

The radishes grumble, 'We're stuck underground!'
But they giggle and wriggle, making quite a sound.
The peas make jokes that are sheer delight,
As the flowers laugh till they lose their height.

In this patch of cheer, all plants have a say,
Creating a laugh on a sunny day.
With roots intertwining, they fashion a crew,
Just waiting to prank those who wander through.

Echoes of Daylight in the Fertile Field

When the crows gather, 'tis a humorous rally,
They squawk like old men in a friendly valley.
The corn stalks gossip about the best dress,
While pumpkins boast of their roundness no less.

Cucumbers twist like they've hit a grand show,
Competing for laughs in the garden glow.
A scarecrow grins, with hat askew,
While dreaming of dancing, in a field of blue.

The beans tell tales of their climb up the fence,
While beets cha-cha, it's pure garden suspense.
Mice munching on crumbs, oh what a feast,
As they host a picnic—their laughter released!

With sunlight weaving through each leafy friend,
All join the fun, from beginning to end.
In this playful patch, where laughter does yield,
The echoes of joy dance across the field.

Glimmers of Hope in the Dark Brown

Beneath the surface, worms wiggle with glee,
While radishes ponder, 'Are we meant to be?'
The soil's deep secrets, a ticklish affair,
They giggle and wiggle without a care.

The ants form a line for their daily parade,
Confidently stepping, in sunshine they wade.
"Watch us!" they chant, "We're working so hard,
But still, here we stand, not one but a yard!"

Mushrooms, like hats, pop up with a grin,
Whispering rumors of what lies within.
"The roots hold the stories, both funny and wise,
Like the clumsy old tree that dreams to rise!"

As laughter erupts from beneath the brown crust,
Each bump and each wrinkle, a giggle to trust.
With every new sprout, a fresh giggly veil,
In this earthy world, it's never too pale.

The Secret Life Beneath the Bright

The ants throw a party, so lively and loud,
While earthworms shimmy, so vibrant and proud.
'Tis the underground circus, with tiny applause,
As the beetles tap dance without any laws.

Fungi salute as they puff up with flair,
In a game of hide and seek, the roots take the dare.
'If you can't see us, we must be quite neat!'
Said the potatoes, feeling fancy down deep in their seat.

The snails on a mission, oh what a slow race,
Take their time, leaving trails all over the place.
"Gotta savor the journey!" they gleefully chant,
While wishing each leaf might sprout them a plant.

Under this blanket, where laughter connects,
Every critter is busy, what fun it reflects.
So here's to the fun of the life 'neath the sun,
Where roots twist and tumble, we know it's all fun!

Harvests of Daybreak

Woke up with a tickle, a giggle, a grin,
My veggies are dancing, let the fun begin!
Carrots wear hats, turnips show glee,
Radishes twirl like they're at a spree.

The tomatoes are blushing, giving a wink,
As peas in their pods start to clink and blink.
Gathering laughter from rows in a rush,
With garlic that whispers, "Oh, what a crush!"

Corn is a saxophone, playing its tune,
While broccoli dons a big, leafy balloon.
The cucumbers giggle, rolling in glee,
Harvesting joy is as fun as can be!

So come join the circus, the harvest parade,
Where every green sprite is a funny charade.
They'll tell you the secrets of how to be tall,
And dance like a dandy, in beanbag ball!

Shimmering Essence Beneath

Beneath the surface, a party's in line,
With worms doing the worm, feeling just fine.
Tiny sprouts gossiping, sharing their dreams,
While roots sing a song, or so it seems.

Cabbage rolls over, says, "Watch me dance,"
What a leafy delight, in a whimsy romance!
Peppers wear sequins, all flashy and bright,
As radish rings twinkle with pure delight.

"Don't dig too deep! You'll ruin the fun!"
A chorus of seedlings starts to run.
The beetroot is blushing, so shy in the mix,
While onions trade stories of clever little tricks.

So if you stoop low, and sparkle your cheer,
You'll find the bright giggles that lie hidden near.
Join the romp down below, oh what a sight,
With roots full of laughter - let's party tonight!

The Lullaby of Growth

As night cloaks the garden, a soft, silly hum,
The sprouts yawn and stretch, oh, here they come!
They whisper their dreams, in the cool night air,
While fireflies twinkle like they just don't care.

"Let's grow a parade of the wackiest things!"
Says bean to the corn, as it does silly swings.
"Don't forget the tomatoes, dressed up all red,
With leafy old cabbages on crowns for their heads!"

Mushrooms pop out, wearing hats just for fun,
While herbs shake their leaves under the moonrun.
The carrots laugh loud, in their cozy tight beds,
They dream of the pranks that they'll pull on their heads.

So drift into dreams, where the plants come to play,
Where the giggles of growth light up the pathway.
In the quiet of night, when all's sleepy and still,
The lullaby of antics gives a cheerful thrill!

Beams in the Garden

In the garden plot, a light-hearted scene,
Where zucchinis sprout with a flair so obscene.
Lettuce lounges low, like it's on a retreat,
While beets write their memoirs from the comfy seat.

The sun peeks in, with a cheeky grin,
As basil spins pirouettes, oh where to begin?
Chives throw a party, with roots tapping beat,
While peas in a pod huddle up, oh so sweet.

The pumpkins are polishing their orange-hued skin,
And garlic takes selfies with a cheeky chin.
The radishes bask in the rays so divine,
"Oh, life is a game, with a laugh and a line!"

So come to the haven, where silliness grows,
Where life's just a dance and the garden still glows.
With each sprout and bloom, let the antics unfold,
In this patch of pure joy, a story retold!

Morning's Warmth on Fertile Loam

A wiggly worm danced in the dirt,
With a tiny hat, it wore a flirty skirt.
The daisies giggled, heads held high,
As a squirrel complained about a pie in the sky.

Chickens clucked about how to strut,
While rabbits argued on who's more nutty and cut.
The breeze whispered secrets, funny and bright,
While the soil chuckled with sheer delight.

A potato played tag with a trotting beet,
Using a carrot's green as a clever cheat.
All this mischief under the morning's flair,
Without a care, just a whimsical air.

Laughter erupted as a crow lost a race,
To a wobbly snail, at a very slow pace.
Oh, what a morning for creatures to play,
In the warm embrace of this funny ballet.

Dances of Light and Land

A beetle wore shades, looking oh so cool,
While the flowers just blushed, breaking every rule.
The ants threw a party, with crumbs for their feast,
While a wise old tortoise claimed he's the least.

The shadows were laughing, just full of cheer,
As the grasshoppers boasted, 'We hop far and near!'
A butterfly slipped on a paint-splattered shoe,
And tripped on a stem as if it knew what to do.

Beneath the soft glow, a dance floor emerged,
As worms tangled up, their enthusiasm surged.
With giggles and wiggles, they shuffled about,
Creating a spectacle, leaving no doubt.

Crickets chirped a tune, catchy and light,
While the blooms twisted 'round, oh what a sight!
In this festive realm, let the joy expand,
With nature's own jigs in this jolly land.

Nature's Luminous Tapestry

A crafty raccoon with a sparkly cap,
Thought he could sneak in for a quick, silly nap.
But the mushrooms all giggled, and summoned a breeze,
As they flicked at his tail: 'We're not here to please!'

An owl hooted loudly, 'This isn't your zone!'
While the daisies protested, 'We want it alone!'
The day was a spectacle of funny mishaps,
With creatures and critters all sharing their snaps.

A lizard in shades took a sunbake so bold,
While the ants all debated whose treasure is gold.
Each leaf had a story, each breeze a cheer,
In this radiant fabric, laughter drew near.

The butterflies fluttered, giggling with glee,
As they swirled around singing, 'Come dance with me!'
In a world so amusing, full of surprises,
They spun and they swooped, amidst all the rises.

The Glistening Veins of the World

A puddle reflected the sun's silly grin,
As frogs played hopscotch, they knew they'd win.
With splashes and plops, their laughter rang out,
While a dragonfly giggled, 'What's that all about?'

The bees wore bow ties, as they buzzed with style,
While flowers convened for a gossiping while.
'The tulips know secrets we just can't repeat!'
Old daisies winked slyly, 'Now isn't this neat?'

Squiggly roots tangled in a humorous game,
As the sunbeams sparkled, never feeling lame.
Earthworms claimed they were winning the race,
While fungus chimed in with a grin on its face.

And so in this realm of giggles and grin,
Nature's own jesters let the fun begin.
With laughter aplenty and joy set in motion,
The glistening veins held a whimsical notion.

Birth of Flora in a Radiant Embrace

A daisy said to a wandering bee,
"Would you like some honey? It's quite the spree!"
The rose, eavesdropping, giggled with glee,
"Just don't get stuck in that sticky decree!"

In the dance of the daisies, oh what a sight,
They twirled and they whirled, oh what pure delight!
The tulips were gossiping, oh such a fright,
They claimed the violets were prancing at night!

A marigold whispered with cheeky finesse,
"Why do the weeds always try to impress?"
The sun chuckled back, "They're just a hot mess!"
As petals burst forth, in sheer happiness!

In this garden of laughter, no worries here,
Where blooms are like jokes and smiles draw near.
Each flower a punchline, bringing us cheer,
A florid parade, let's all give a cheer!

Roots that Drink from Luminous Casks

The roots had a party, oh what a rave,
Sipping from pools, where the moisture was brave.
"Watch out! Here comes a worm, looking to scave!"
Laughter erupted, as the leaves did wave.

A carrot brought snacks, all crunchy and bright,
"These radishes just won't share, what a sight!"
The potatoes chimed in, "Join us for a bite!"
And all of them danced till the fall of night.

The parsley stood tall, wearing shades made of grass,
"I'm cooler than mint—sure that's a real class!"
The basil just swooned, in a versy green mass,
As roots drank together, the good vibes amassed.

As night closed in like a cozy warm quilt,
They made plans for a parade, built with good wit.
To gather the sunlight, each day they were lit,
Those roots and their revels, they truly legit!

Gardens Bathed in Ethereal Hues

In a garden so wacky with colors and laughs,
The flowers debated their fanciest shafts.
"Look at my petals, they're bold, not like half!"
But daisies made jokes, gave the roses a scaf.

"Oh, lavender, dear, see how periwinkle chimes,
Don't you wish you could twirl, without any crimes?"
The violets just snickered, "We're passing the rhymes,
And let's not forget about those mimes with thyme."

As butterflies fluttered, all dressed up in flair,
They held a grand contest for who'd get the air.
The blooms looked so pleased, oh so debonair,
While worms rolled their eyes, just lying in despair.

When the sun dipped low and the stars took their cue,
The petals all huddled, for warmth, and for brew.
With laughter and friendship, they flourished anew,
In a garden where giggles and colors just grew!

Celestial Variations of Grounded Love

In a patch of green, where the critters convene,
The daisies declared, "We're the best of the scene!"
The hyacinths laughed, "You're smelling quite keen,
But we're the real stars, if you know what I mean!"

The ferns reminisced of their glorious sprawl,
"We've stood here the longest, we're having a ball!"
But a curious squirrel scoffed, "You stand so small,
In the world of grand dreams, we just in the hall!"

Suddenly a breeze made the petals all sway,
They twinkled and winked, in their colorful way.
As moonlight cascaded in shimmering play,
They agreed, in this chaos, laughter would stay.

So here's to the blooms, in a world full of cheer,
With funny remarks and a chortle or jeer.
They bloom for each other, so close and so near,
In gardens of giggles, forever sincere!

www.ingramcontent.com/pod-product-compliance
Lightning Source LLC
Chambersburg PA
CBHW072127070526
44585CB00016B/1563